ALL ABOUT STELANS

ALL ABOUT STELANS

PARIS TOSEN

CANADA

This is a book of nonfiction.

First edition, March 2016
Revised edition, May 2016
Second edition, July 2016

Some contents also published in the book *The Earth-Colonizing Handbook of Generation Stelan* (2016)

ISBN 978-1-530796-80-9 (pbk)
ISBN 978-1-988014-15-9 (ebook)

Book design by the author

www.stelan.ca

STARMAN (1984)–

Jenny Hayden: What's it like up there?

Starman: It is beautiful. Not like this, but it is beautiful. There is only one language, one law, one people. There is no war, no hunger. The strong do not victimize the helpless. We are very civilized, but we have lost something, I think. You are all so much alive, all so different.

Contents

AUTHOR'S NOTE

This book is based on a series of video-based discussions that contradict the fundamental beliefs about the nature of human beings and their relationship with advanced interstellar cultures. That globalized and concretized understanding of human origins, perpetually ingrained into our conscious and subconscious over centuries of cultural programming, repetition, and biblical dedications, is now a human standard. But, in my judgement, it is an ancient standard that has simply been repeated and duplicated throughout human history. And it is fundamentally misguided. It lacks the essential component and virtual springboard to explain the birth of the first humans.

This book aims, in a succinct way, to reconstruct those missing essentials of human history, relying on the misappropriation of interstellar and interdimensional people.

I am neither a scientist nor an anthropologist. I hold no credentials in colonization and I hold no training in the disciplines associated with astronomy. My bachelor's degree is in Business Administration with majors in International Business and Marketing.

Ironically, the knowledge presented in this book could never have come from any of those disciplines (or experts) above because the topic of "extraterrestrials" has been terribly censored, suppressed, and classified for a very long time. For many citizens, the topic is purely fictional. Instead, I speak from experience, that is, direct experience and a great amount of research on the topics of interest.

I never approached this strange field from the usual UFO investigation route. I didn't do that because my first direct encounter with offplanet cultures happened to be interdimensional Elves. I was 38 when it happened and the result changed the direction of my life.

I didn't need to find UFOs to prove that ETs existed because the "ETs" entered my apartment three nights in a row (and I wrote about it). I knew that we were not alone. What I didn't understand was who these people were and what they wanted. That started me on a cultural exploration unlike ever before.

Fortunately, I had a strong background in intercultural communication primarily from my background in Asian culture, with a heavy focus on the Chinese culture.

For 20 years, I had taken a keen interest in Chinese culture—food, fashion, Kung Fu, Traditional Chinese Medicine, philosophy, history, language—so much so that I went on to study Chinese history, Mandarin Chinese, and foreign market entry at university.

Central to understanding any foreign people is making sense of their culture. Who are they? How do they think? What is important to them? What is their history like? What kinds of tribulations have they endured and why?

After graduation, I moved to Hong Kong where I worked for a couple of years before moving to Shanghai, China, a place I would stay for four years. This self-guided cultural immersion program would provide the bulk of my cross-cultural training that I would later use to understand interstellar and interdimensional cultures.

When I moved to Shanghai on Boxing Day in 1998, I had no money, no friends, no job, and I couldn't speak Mandarin. My language training from university was barely sufficient for a tourist.

China, unlike most people think of the country, is an ethnically diverse nation with over 50 different ethnicities throughout the Mainland. Every city you go to they speak a different dialect, they dress different, they cook different, and they have different customs.

Twenty years of cultural training would, odd as it seems, provide the cornerstone for my approach to Stelan Peoples. After a number of books on the subject of Stelans, and their sciences, I wanted to write a more succinct volume and chose my video material as the basis because it summed up perfectly what I wanted to say.

In my opinion, one of my main issues on the subject of extraterrestrials is the rampant anti-alien sentiment. What most people still don't know is that propagandists and experts in psychological operations ("psy-ops") were handed the task of betraying the masses, especially noticeable in the United States. "Aliens," "extraterrestrials," "extraterrestrial biological entities," "space monsters" – all military and intelligence terms designed to distance the public from genuine Stelan cultures.

Rather than argue against the betrayal, this personal book fills in the historical gaps necessary for people to move forward. It is a small book about a very big topic. It is an expanded view of reality from a man who has experienced a very different kind of reality.

Paris Tosen

INTRODUCTION
HIDDEN HISTORY

The history of humankind is incomplete. I think its incompleteness stems from a multi-century old plan to suppress, cover-up, disgorge, misinform and to classify "Top Secret" anything having to do with the subject of nonhumans. The presence of advanced interstellar and interdimensional cultures on, near, and inside the Earth—as far-fetched and absurd as that might have once seemed, is now well-within a plausible reality.

  The history that society has been fed has been vehemently and woefully redacted to protect an elite powerbase, a Cabal, whose only intention was to secure the masthead for the planet. And this process of redaction, although has become crueler and more excessive in the most recent 100 years, it has been ongoing for thousands of years. That is to say, elite societies have kept in secret what advanced cultures, from other galaxies and star systems, have provided to them on an ongoing

7

basis all for the sole purpose of providing the prerequisite for global domination.

We are on the cusp of a new dawn in human history whereby the true history of this planet will increasingly become available. That new history will be revealed alongside the arrival and presence of interstellar and interdimensional cultures, verily races of people that most of us have only witnessed in fictional stories.

Stelan Peoples, the category for describing these advanced races—because a race of beings having technologies a million years ahead of us should be considered advanced—have often been termed "aliens" and "extraterrestrials," a form of military discrimination that maligned any genuine contact attempts.

The atrocities that this Cabal committed with top-notch alien secrets and aid from disenfranchised criminal ETs is immeasurable and will eventually be made available to some degree. The secret history of the United States, and may other powerful nations—since superpower status doesn't form without some extraterrestrial incentive—is going to cause a societal reformation, the likes of which happens every few centuries.

We are at that point in human history, and not to magnify the case of the United States any further than necessary, where the alien support system starts to fall apart and in its place a greater understanding and connection to the universe springs forth.

The (eventual) arrival of genuine starships and the appearance of various nonhuman races, including those that mostly look human, is going to have a profound effect on every nation on this planet. The actual history of humankind will need to be completely rewritten, including our attachments to the Creator belief system.

Let's just be as straight as possible here: We've all been living a myth. This myth did not arise out of accident or casual neglect, rather it formed out of a purposeful plan to sequester the bulk of the human race and to render the global population out of the final equation. If you were to ask me, the plan, the final plan, was to let the masses decay, and worse, to wipe their numbers down to such a level that they wouldn't be troublesome.

I began speaking about interstellar cultures in 2006, shortly after I was visited by three interstellar Elves. The beginnings of my talks and teachings were surrounded by negativity, skepticism, and outright rejection. In fact, up until this point, the masses cannot accept that we are not alone in the universe. And they have every right not to—they've been brainwashed and hypnotized by professionals for more than seven decades.

If you take a 16-year-old, he or she has grown up on alien movies and video games whereby the alien, for the most part, is evil and likely a monster hell-bent on destroying humans. The alien is a galactic threat. Aside from movies like James Cameron's "Avatar" (2009) and John Carpenter's 1982 classic "Starman," the bulk of Hollywood films on the subject denigrate and discriminate with impunity.

But the teenager has nowhere to look for the truth. If they ask their parents, who were brainwashed their entire lives on evil ETs, they get nothing. The grandparents grew up with repeated viewings of the "War of the Worlds" material. But the mass mind control program was not by happenstance, it was well planned by those proficient in psychological operations.

A psy-op requires direction and operational goals that must be achieved in order to become a success. It also requires a team of professional operatives, even if those operatives work undercover. People do not easily surrender what they believe with a good amount of propaganda and that propaganda amounts to mass hypnosis. In order to achieve its seismic goals of total population control, a militarized intelligence unit must work clandestinely.

The idea that society could not prove the existence of extraterrestrials on its own, or that there weren't enough real images of UFOs that passed a discriminating eye, only congratulates the effects of these secret military operations. Since the establishment of the National Security Act in 1947, just 18 days after a flying saucer was shot down over Roswell, New Mexico, the psychological agents had every intention to destroy the UFO field and to bury the extraterrestrial discussion.

The result of information sequestration, document and media censorship, ostracism of high profile researchers, and classifying all materials on ETs Top Secret, the UFO field has fallen apart save a few ragtag individuals, people who just can't let it go, and who have paid the cost of belief in otherworldly things.

In the Information Age, the cost to maintain an effective psy-ops on UFOs and ETs has become unreasonable and the ability to shut off activists and their information, even leaked information, has declined. The internet has allowed a new level of information dissemination on the extraterrestrial topic unlike ever before. Prior to the Information Age, my own work and ideas, perhaps even myself, would have been killed off and blocked any media access. Indeed, some who came close to public acceptance sadly died prematurely.

This small book covers a handful of some very important topics having to do with Stelan People, anyone with an offplanet heritage. In it I provide a new explanation for human origins, from my personal view, and detail the emergence of Generation Stelan, a genetically distinct race of people that is an evolutionary leap from human beings. This book contains a collection of my video discussions on Stelan cultures, and relies on my opinions on these topics.

You should find information here that you are not familiar with because it speaks about the redacted portions of human history, as I understand. Although not a full book the information is very much relatable and useful. It is succinct by design. Stelans are no longer just thoughts and images in the sky, rather we are their extended families, their descendants and their offspring, and soon enough we'll see them again.

Paris Tosen

ELVES MAKE HOUSE CALLS

Everyone goes through life and has all kinds of experiences. We have travel experiences. We have romantic experiences. We have life-changing experiences. Well, in 2005, I had a life-changing experience. One which I would never have anticipated. I was 38 years old at the time—yes, do the math. And my life wasn't going particularly well, but it felt as if a period of my life had changed. I had gone through a cycle, I suppose, and things were calming down and I was deciding what to do next with my life, at this stage, and that's when I had an experience and what really allowed me to go through this experience was the fact that I had a very vivid imagination.

I'm a writer. I been writing for nearly 25 years. I have a pretty strong imagination. Sometimes my imagination gets the best of me and I get myself into the wrong situations, but, for the most part, the art in writing requires you to be open-minded. Closeminded people don't do very well in creative pursuits.

So it was in 2005, in November, when I met three very strange men. Now they were very strange men because they happened to come from another dimension. I can speak about it now, being 10 years later, in a calm, rational way, but that experience was a life-changing experience and it took me many years to understand, to translate, and to figure out; and that led to a whole revamp, a reboot of my life; and the readjustment to society, and all the questions came up—hundreds of thousands of questions came up as to why was this happening, who were these people, what did they want, why me?

I'm not going to discuss those things today. I just want to share the experience of these three strange men that came into my bachelor suite.

They came into my bachelor suite in Vancouver. I was just living off of Broadway Street & Granville Street and it is not known for any strange happenings there. It is not a UFO "hot spot." There's no witchcraft there. There is no circle of power, Ley Lines. It's just a place in the city.

So, there's no indication of anything coming. There's no reason for anything coming. Certainly myself, the last thing on my mind is what happened—and what happened was about mid-

November in the middle of the night, two or three in the morning, I am on my computer, I'm sitting there doing some research.

At about this time of my life, I'm looking for alternative information. Ten years ago there wasn't that much alternative information, but that's when I felt behind me was like a wave of energy entered the room.

It's almost like you're in a pool of water and then there's a big wave of water that passes through you, or under you, and you can feel that wave of water, right? When you go to the beach you can feel the waves of water, but you can also see the water.

Well, in my particular case I could see there was no water, there was energy. Water is synonymous with energy in the field of cosmic knowledge. It's a good analogy. This wave of energy entered into my pool of existence. I was calm about it because you feel energy all the time, you try not to make a big exaggeration of it. Try not to get hysterical.

Again, my reaction is quite different than most people, especially in the past who tend to react negatively, that tend to be afraid, that tend to think of ghosts and goblins and bad omens and stuff like that.

I tend to have more positive outcomes. I'm more positive minded and I'm open to these kinds of wild things happening. So, I turn around in my chair—again, I'm not expecting, anything—and I see coming through a portal, basically the walls. They are coming out of the walls; my bachelor suite is one room. They are basically coming through the air. Three figures—one, two, three—they are very tall.

Again, at this time my vision; my understanding is very poor. So I'm going to use some of my realizations *after* the fact—that they were quite tall. They had very sharp features. They were very well dressed. At the time I thought of them as swashbucklers. They were like wearing swashbuckling clothes. "The Count of Monte Cristo" and "The Three Musketeers"—kind of this wild fashion, exotic fashion, slightly to that level, but they weren't pirates, they weren't swashbucklers. But there were three tall figures. To my third eye, if I use my third eye (some people have second sight) I can see three men.

This is the middle the night. I'm not thinking, "Is this a hallucination?" I'm not thinking they're there to hurt me, because I didn't feel that. They felt friendly. They presented themselves as men of class, intelligent, so I stood up, not looking at these three interdimensional beings in my apartment in Vancouver.

Now I don't do drugs. I've *never* done drugs; I really don't drink that much. I don't do any weird hallucinogenics. I drink coffee, stuff like that. Normal stuff. Pretty normal stuff. At the time I was lucid, it was normal. I was calm. They were calm. I said okay this is interesting. They immediately started to communicate with me using telepathy. Telepathy is just communication by mind or thought.

The problem was they were communicating using a different language. They were using some kind of offplanet interdimensional language and my human self couldn't translate it, but there was a part of me that could understand. And there was a part of me that felt familiar with these people, these three strange men whom I later called Elves.

Elves are these interdimensional people. They live in other dimensions and they can travel to our dimension. They may appear in physical form. In my particular case, for my particular reason, they appeared to me in kind of a *hazy* physical form. In other words, they didn't fully appear in the visible spectrum. They were partially cloaked but I could see them so they wouldn't have to present themselves in a visible spectrum because actually I could see them because I had second sight; I had some kind of—in the old times they called it "second sight"—or third eye.

Some people have this natural ability. I found out I have this ability. They said a bunch of things and then they spoke to me in English, the last little bit, because they knew the human person didn't understand and with that after about twenty minutes they left. Now I thought to myself, okay that was strange; that was interesting.

Again, I didn't turn it into a negative. I didn't become afraid, which is the standard response. I didn't all of a sudden say something bad. It was an atypical response. And then I went back to my computer.

Was it a hallucination? Well, the next night I felt that energy—I was on my computer again—I felt that wave of energy, I turn around sooner this time and I saw them walking through a portal through the air. Some kind of interdimensional portal.

Now my mind is thinking, well, do hallucinations happen twice, the same way, the same time of day and night? I wasn't taking anything. I was lucid. They presented themselves in the same way. Now it's like seeing somebody for the second time. They communicated with me in an *offplanet language* of which I seemed to understand—that was the bulk of the communication—and then the last part was a little bit in English. So after that happened, they went away. I saw them go through the portal. I saw these people go through the portal, the energy in the room shifted. The wave of energy left and the room changed back to its original state.

These were visible. These things you could feel, that you could see. You could get sort-of the atmosphere and the vibe of the room. All of this is shifting when they come in and when they go out. I'm thinking twice in a row, there's something going on here.

The next night—so three nights in a row—they came back; did the same thing. Can it be a hallucination? They said the same thing in their language. They said the same thing in English, which later prompted me to seek out this psychic intuitive which I discussed and wrote about.

Now, do hallucinations happen in this manner? Do hallucinations communicate to you using telepathy? This kind of telepathy was a very clear voice in my head like a radio that was clear, sharp, lucid. There were no derogatory remarks. They were very intelligent and it wasn't coming for me; and there's three of them so there were some shared thoughts.

So now by the third time, I said to myself this is not something that happens every day. This is not something that is an induced hallucination. This is not an attack. This is not an abduction. This is not all these things; "it is not" business it's intelligent. These are people, they are not monsters. They're intelligent. They present themselves intelligently but I decided from those experiences in 2005 that these people had made an effort to traverse the dimensions to find me, and I said to myself, "There's got to be a reason for that and the things they said I tried to understand, but there had to be a reason for that. I mean this is not an accident."

Three times in a row they came to talk to me. They needed to talk to me. Well, at the time I didn't think I was that special, b) I didn't know anybody in the other dimension. I didn't know any Stelans (aliens); I didn't know anything.

But, I decided they made the effort to find me and they communicated with me so if somebody makes an effort three times—to come from another dimension—I felt it was my obligation to make the effort to find out what they wanted, and one of the things they said was "they have trouble communicating with me" and I needed to fix that. And if I could fix that then I could communicate with them and they could communicate more; we can have more communication because there were a lot of questions. So I said to myself, I felt obligated (they made the effort), I made the effort to resolve that communication problem and that process changed my life, but for the better.

Well, on a personal side, maybe not the better, but in terms of why I'm here, what I'm doing, what's my work about, it's better. It is the right thing.

It was the right thing to do and what they did had a lot of meaning. By the same token, I had to make the effort. So these things had to work in tandem. They made the effort and I didn't freak out. I didn't run away. I didn't start screaming "abduction" or "cattle mutilation."

And I made a sincere effort and that profoundly changed my life and it's shaped the last 10 years of my life. The three Elves. Do I believe in other dimensions? Yes. Why do I believe? Because I have the correct life-changing experience. Now most people don't have that kind of experience and there were many other experiences following that (experience), but is it a belief or is it because you saw something, right? So that was my experience with the three Elves. They live in the other dimensions because we live in a multidimensional world and one day we'll figure that out.

EARTH COLONY

We have a relatively important discussion to make and it has to do with space colonization, and it also has to do with indigenous cultures and it has to do with the human culture. So what are these three things? How are they connected because there's this belief, there's this predication, predilection *that* the "human being" is indigenous to this planet. That's a fundamental belief stemming back from ancient times to the fossil evidence, human fossil evidence dating back several million years, suggesting that the human race evolved (evolution) from a primate into the modern human, into the neo-human, into the Stelan; and this is, I would say, this is a fundamental belief that spans many cultures in many nations and many people. Therefore, the conclusion is that because human beings apparently evolved, or were created— doesn't matter the explanation—they stem (originate) from this planet called Earth (*terra firma*).

But that means that because humans originated from the Earth, they are the indigenous culture, i.e. the native culture, i.e. the original culture, the original species. So, we say that humans are an indigenous race and we look at the aboriginal cultures in the early native cultures as our forebears. Our forefathers. Our ancestors. So that our ancient ancestors, you know, were natives. Our ancient, ancient ancestors were primates and other primitive life forms: Homo-erectus and Australopithecus, so on and so forth. But that runs contrary to the actual situation that says that we are a Space Colony.

That the human genome, the human genus, originated from other parts of the universe; be it another solar system, another star system, another galaxy, another planet or set of planets. A series of planets. And that genomic data, which constitutes the human being was brought *here* to create the human species.

So, colonization, maybe it's because we haven't done it as a race yet, it's mysterious and speculative and always provocative—it's provocative, well we haven't done it—because we haven't done it does not mean that it has not been done before by other advanced societies, other advanced cultures inhabiting the universe.

I'm of the opinion, and I've been convinced, and I have been discussing it for nearly 10 years, that there are other cultures (Stelan cultures) that inhabit other parts of the universe and are even here in this solar system on or near this planet. So, there's no argument there on my part. That influences my understanding of the way things are, rather than the conventional thinking of evolution or creation. My thinking—from my other knowledge—is that this planet was colonized.

There are several ways to colonize a planet. I'm not an expert in space colonization, unfortunately, but these are some ideas that we can work with: a) Somebody from another system travels here with some DNA specimens, i.e. some proto-human, and they genetically engineer it using the available DNA here, even corn DNA and the DNA from bananas and trees; and squirrels and fish, frogs, whatever; they combine that proto-DNA, which they brought, with some of the DNA here to create (engineer) a proto-human.

The proto-human evolves. The engineers, the geneticists from afar; they come back bringing more DNA and they combine it with the protohumans they've created 1,000 years ago and they create a new generation of the human. They go away, they come back. You get the idea.

They periodically bring additional DNA from their lab and they combine it; they engineer a new *genus*: hence there are these evolutionary leaps from a primate to a proto-human, Cro-Magnon, Neanderthal, Homo sapiens, etc., so that evolution does take place on some level, but this evolution is greatly modified through genetic engineering. That's one form of space colonization.

The second idea is that *in addition to* this "evolutionary track" other human beings from other planets migrated to Earth and they formed colonies and cultures, even nations later on, that cohabited, coexisted with the DNA of that engineered proto-human that became Human X; and then the migrants also then they procreated and then they were maybe engineered; they coexisted. And then there are other migrants, maybe from other star systems and other planets, who looked human, and they migrated to this planet. So all of this immigration created what we can now see as the multicultural indigenous race. Because think about it: if you had one proto-human primate how would you get an African, an Asian, a Caucasian—from one (set of genes) right?

There's lots of logical problems with this but this is my understanding. This is with the understanding that there are Stelan cultures. There are advanced races. There are people in other star systems and other parts of the universe, in other galaxies, even in other universes. Even in other dimensions and they have been traveling here and they have influenced not only, you know, nature; they've also been involved in the engineering of the race, the modification—to such an extent that we are not the indigenous race, which is my basic conclusion that human beings are not indigenous to Earth.

We'd like to believe that. Many people *do* believe that, they will go to their grave believing that, but I come from the understanding that you can colonize a planet using many methods. I've given you a couple of methods in simple (in summary) that you can bring DNA here, you can migrate here, you can even have the people here and then you can modify and engineer their children so the child can be born of a proto-human and then you can have an engineered human born from the child.

There are many ways scientifically, and I'm not a scientist even, there are many ways to genetically engineer, modify species using human modern scientific methods, and not even thinking about advanced methods, that can do things between dimensions. That can do things at a distance. You could e-mail, if you could e-mail DNA to the planet from another system—as a speculative idea here— you can e-mail DNA into the species here and the child will be a genetically modified person. Without ever having to travel to the planet, you can modify the DNA or the DNA sequences.

Just like on a computer, you go on a computer and you can go online and you can change the computer code and that updates the website. So imagine you can go; you can use a computer to modify the DNA and then you can *up-change*, you can update, the code of the species of the human being, of the animal, of the tree; simply by using, maybe not a standard computer, but by using a special computer (machine) to genetically modify and update different things here including the race of people or specific people or specific races of people. To such an extent that through evolution we are indistinguishable, we look the same—there's a *homogeneity* among human beings even though we have smaller ears or slanted eyes or smaller noses or bigger noses; black hair, white hair, blonde hair, we accept the notion that we're all human, but really, all these things can be modified through genetic modification, through genetic sequencing, through genetic engineering; and all of it is controlled through the DNA.

If the DNA is thought of as "software," you only have to understand how to manipulate genetic software and maybe not the early stages but the later stages, you can just, you know, Dial-A-Species basically.

It's not difficult to colonize a planet, although human beings haven't done it yet; other species, other races, have done it, and some of them look human and, so, therefore we are living in a Space Colony.

Welcome to Colony Earth.

Paris Tosen

THE EARTH COLONIZATION PROGRAM

The subject of today's matter is moving forward. That is the theme of my life. It is moving forward, and it is the theme of humanity; it is the theme of any existential being; is the theme of the human civilization what we call "human-kind" because humankind has grown to this point, this stage, under certain pre-assumptions (assumptions), certain forms of limited education as to the nature of our origins; as to the nature of our ancestry.

Now, as I've said before, Earth is a colony. Earth is a Space Colony. Now what does that mean? That means a) There are other colonies that predate earth; there other colonies, b) There are colonization civilizations; there are colonists and colonizers. In order to qualify as a colonizer, you have to be more advanced than the planet that you colonize. This is no different than the Spanish conquistadors traveling to South America, to the south of North America, and interacting with the aboriginals and colonizing South America and what is now Mexico. Mexicans speak Spanish because of Spain and Canada, on the Eastern Coast, we speak French because of French colonists. English is the central language of North America because of British colonists.

So if you say to yourself, "Well, I am from this country," yes, but, who came before you and who left their imprint in your language, in your genetic history, in your blood. It is not you who originated it, rather it is the colonists.

On a larger scale, Earth was colonized by advanced agencies, advanced civilizations. Now the concept is not difficult understand. The concept— because we've seen colonization we know that even in North America, the British, the French and the Spanish came over and wiped out the aboriginals, most of the aboriginals, especially American Indians who've been ritualistically exterminated and then given these allotments, these reservations, and were told to stay there and shut up or we will go in there with the Army and we will put you down, which they did for hundreds of years.

Colonization is well understood. What is not understood is the scale. The problem is the scale because we are used to countries. We are used to cultures and nations. We don't understand planetary colonization because that information has been blocked off. That information is not discussed in the history books because that information has been censored, has been completely suppressed.

It has been suppressed and one of the ways to suppress it is to create the "alien space monster," such that, anything from outer space is an alien space monster that wants to commit planetary genocide. They are mass murderers, serial killers; they want to eat your babies; they are exploding out of your chest; there's going to be a huge alien invasion. So that specter is outer space; therefore, you don't think about outer space.

This is classic mind control, the bogeyman. You tell your child there's a bogeyman outside and the child will not want to go outside, will not want to think to go outside. They will lock themselves in the room and they will never come out because there is a bogeyman, don't go there. This is a classic story that's been used for centuries. There's a monster there, don't go there.

There is no monster.

It's called mind control. It's brainwash.

The same thing.

So the agencies said, "There's a bogeyman in space,"

Then they create these movies: "There's going to be an invasion. They're going to wipe us out."

"If there is an intelligent race out there, they're going to wipe out the human race."

That's the mind control/brainwash. It is brainwash because if you've done your research, if you're educated, you understand that we are a colony. We were colonized. We are the children of those colonists.

Look at yourself: Do you look like a space monster? Ask yourself, look at the mirror, do you look like a space monster? Do you want to commit mass genocide? Are you a mass murderer? No. But if you are the product of these races of people from outer space and you're not a monster and you don't have tentacles coming out of your ass, right, then does that mean that your forebears, your ancestors, are like-minded—that they're not evil monsters, that there's not going to be an invasion, right; so this is the link because if we are the result of a colonization and as human beings we're decent—most of us are decent human beings, we're intelligent, we're compassionate, we're understanding, we seek knowledge; we raise our children like that.

If we are the product of these interstellar colonists, then the interstellar colonists are not monsters. The interstellar colonists are not space invaders and they don't have tentacles growing out of their ass because we don't have tentacles growing out of our ass; and that's what's been suppressed.

"There's a bogeyman space, don't think about space. If you think space, think about bacteria, think about the stars, ooh there's Jupiter."

There are people there because there are people here. *There are people here.* And some of these civilizations that came here are *still here*—both on the Earth, in the Earth, and above the Earth—and they look human.

You know why they *look* human? Because the human genome (human DNA) did not originate from here. It was not created by some guy on a magic cloud.

It has been influenced by geneticists who came from advanced civilizations. So, as the human civilization needs to move forward, we need to come to terms with this reality.

The reality is we are the *children* of interstellar colonists who, some are still here, and some are near here; some are living among us and this is part of that disclosure.

The disclosure is that we are Space Colony.

Welcome to the Earth Colony.

The people who created us are more advanced than us. This is a fact. This is how they can remain hidden. They are more advanced than us; and, many of them look human. They could walk among society and be invisible because you don't understand—because you're looking for space monsters—you're looking for the evil alien with the tentacle coming out of his ass. And they're walking right in front of you; they are your next-door neighbor and they're human, but they are also from another civilization.

So, it's very simple when you understand that if you have a child the child is human because you are human, right? So, you are human because your parents were human. Your parents were human because your grandparents and great grandparents were human, but if those humans were from other planets who migrated here, who came from under the Earth, who look human, and over time they were adjusted genetically by science—not by a guy on a magic cloud—then everybody looks the same, looks human, but there's different degrees of humanity.

There's the humanity here who understands that there are other civilizations and that they're advanced civilizations and there's humanity here which is you—which you have no clue. Because you're afraid of space monsters. You are afraid to *look* at the *possibility* that aliens (extraterrestrials) look like us.

Now that's not to say, as I finish, that's not to say that all interstellar cultures look human. There is a wide spectrum of cultures, as I've said before. I've written about this. There is a wide spectrum.

Some look very human. Some look not human. Some look like humanoids. Some look like animal humans. Some look completely different. Some are energy. So, there is a wide spectrum, but *we* are the descendants of the human spectrum. Because we don't have tentacles coming out of our ass. If you have a tentacle coming out of your ass, then you come from the Tentacle Coming Out of Their Ass culture.

So, this is the year, as I've said, this is the year—2016 is the year—we open this box of truth, of possibility that space monsters were an illusion implanted, a thought implant, and that we are the descendants of advanced civilizations and they want us to know.

They want you to know. I want you to know because it's important to know where you come from, to know your history. Just like it is important to know that the American Indians and the First Nations were ritualistically abused by their forebears, by our ancestors, but that's not to say every aboriginal was mistreated.

It's important to know where you come from— your history. Your ancestors and our ancestors do not come from the Earth. If they come from the Earth, their ancestors did not come from the Earth, okay.

This is the year, 2016. This is the year. It starts and it will be a process. It will take a number of years before we get this sorted out.

CHILDREN OF KRYPTON

Some people look human, but they're not human.

  When you listen to the news, they don't talk about this subject. When you talk to your friends, they don't talk about this subject. When you watch a movie on aliens and UFOs and extraterrestrials, they tend to focus on the alien invasion. They tend to focus on the Space Monster. They tend to focus of the tentacles and the genocidal maniacs in the motherships. They tend to focus on war and the military, but this is all propaganda.

  This is anti-alien propaganda and the anti-alien propaganda is very heavy. Even if you're in the UFO community there is a lot of disinformation, misinformation, wrong information and, while there may be few nuggets of truth, a lot of stuff is there to scare you. The reason that they want you scared is because as soon as you realize that there are nonhumans on the Earth, that is, humans that look human, but are not human, what I call Stelans, as in stellar humans or interstellar humans, Stelans. As you realize there are Stelans, as soon as you realize they're intelligent and they're scientific and they're technological *and* you realize that they have been here a long time, you come to the natural conclusion that they've been doing something while they were here.

Now the movies and the fearmongers, right, the propagandists, will say they've been abducting and experimenting on people and they've been killing cattle and they're planning an invasion.

That's the propaganda.

But when you step out of that propaganda. When you start to use your brain, you realize intelligent advanced cultures have better things to do than all this stuff, right; all this weird, wild, violent stuff, which is good for entertainment. It's good for the military and intelligence agencies, but is not the truth.

The truth is that when you accept the fact that there are Stelans, then you realize there are Stelan children—offplanet children.

That's a sobering idea, it's a sobering concept that advanced races of people, that may or may not look human, have been involved in a kind of production of children. Creation of children. Now, again, the propagandist will say they've been genetically engineering children and they'll create some kind of scenario where they've enslaved the children genetically. Again that all comes from the disinformation camps and you can tell right away who they are when they sell you this negative, fearful event: implants and the genetic engineering.

My view was different. My view, because my experiences are different, my view is these advanced cultures are scientific cultures, they had every reason and obligation to improve the genetic makeup of this world to increase the genetic biodiversity of the planet. It's a standard in any form of colonization of which Earth is a colony, as any planet. Because if I am here, and someone preceded me, and someone preceded that person, and someone preceded that person. If you go back far enough, there was some kind of migration, right.

Humans will one day go to a different planet and we will colonize that planet and a hundred thousand years later those children will say the same thing we are saying today. So we have our progenitors. We have our ancestors. Our ancestors, like parents, have every intention of producing offspring. You have parents, doesn't matter how old you are, you were genetically engineered through your parents, right.

It's a philosophical discussion. The fact of creating life is a form of genetic engineering and there are scientific ways to do it. Today, we can produce children in test tubes; *in vitro* fertilization, we can implant embryos into a mother. We can implant designer babies into a surrogate mother, which is a different mother from the biological mother. We can genetically modify DNA. We can edit DNA and remove certain traits. We can give children blue eyes, blonde hair; we can do all this. So imagine an advanced culture, they were doing this 5,000 years ago. Why? Because they wanted to create genetic improvements in the population.

My view is that this has been happening for thousands of years. We, today, are the result of tens of thousands of years of generic engineering. Some periods are more intense. Some periods are less intense. My feeling is that anybody under 25 years old, which is born in the late 80s, if you're under 25 years old, you are a Stelan.

In other words, this is human (on one side) and this a Stelan (on the opposite side). You are over here genetically (on the Stelan side).

This raises a lot of questions because why do you look human? Well, what if the human genome (human DNA), what if you came from another planet and they took it from another planet and they say, "Why don't we come to this planet to make *these* people look like *those* people."

So now it's been modified.

Stelans come in different types with different characteristics, which I'll discuss further in the book. If you look under 25 years old and based on the current rates, the demographics of North America, which is Canada, U.S.A., and Mexico (under 25s, 35% of total pop. 474 million), there are about 165 million people, kids, young people aged 25 and under. My view is the 165 million are Stelans and there are several kinds. There's different kinds of Stelans. In other words, we've now moved away from the human genome.

(Which is a profound statement.)

Now again it's like a computer, let's say, the computer can look the same on the outside, but it's the internal mechanics, it's the processor, it's the technology. Same thing with a human being. You can look like a human being, but genetically, you're different, right, genetically different; and it's a longer discussion which we can discuss at a later time. There are 165 million Stelans in North America. What does that mean? It means there's a new culture. There's a Stelan culture.

I want to make this very clear—I'm not talking about an invasion from outer space. I'm not talking about migration from outer space. I'm not talking about little green men or about evil gray beings. I'm talking about aliens that actually are human. But my view is that the human is an alien.

The *original* human genome came from offplanet and we've become accustomed to it, conditioned to it, but actually we are *aliens* and we are *humans*. The next generation of human I call Stelan; improved at the genetic level. The genomic level of which we will understand later on, but we're seeing this already, for example: more sensitivities; more gifts; more talented people; less violent kids. There's a new culture. It's a Stelan culture. There's no reason now for an alien race to invade when most of the world is alien.

If you're older than 25, there's a diminishing rate of return. There's a diminishing Stelan stock, let's say. There were some people modified. There were some people designed, and so forth, but not 100-percent. My view, based on my information and research, is that most of the human race has been modified to one degree or another, and I think this has been done in recent decades. That is to say, an upgrade program started with current adults prior to the 1980s and that program intensified in terms of genetic edits starting in the eighties.

This is why you have this progressive rate of human engineering, and then the shift to a basically Stelan race. But this is my view and I have no genetic evidence to substantiate my theory at this time, although, a small 2 to 5 percent genetic modification is enough to produce an entirely new human species. Plus, those genes may not be easily identified. They may even be shut off to some degree and therefore undetectable.

I prefer the term Stelan, which may not have the same ring as Human, but perhaps in the future it will be a term that makes more sense.

Paris Tosen

SPACE MONSTERS COME FROM HOLLYWOOD

I'm sure all of you have heard about the monsters from outer space. These monsters have tentacles; they have fangs, claws; they have a very bad disposition; they wear biomechanical suits; they, all of them, hate humanity.

They could be spores; they could be insects; they could be trees; viruses; they could be giant creatures made out of all kinds of minerals.

All of these monsters from outer space, aliens we call him. We call them extraterrestrials; they're here to our demise, that is, they're here to wipe out the human race. They eat humans. They're genocidal maniacs. They're homicidal lunatics. They're serial killers. These are the worst of the worst. They're all criminals, according to the movies.

Of course, movies are not documentaries, but that's where the space monster was invented. The space monster was invented in Hollywood. You take the movie like the "Invasion of the Body Snatchers" (1978), based on a movie from the 1950s called the "Body Snatchers." There were these creatures from another planet, they come here and they duplicate our bodies and they replicate and they wipe out the original human in order to take over our world.

In 1979, you have "Alien," which is a very famous movie now, classic, directed by Ridley Scott. "Alien" is this, basically, this hunter killer in a spaceship who eats the entire crew of a ship; and it has acid blood; it has fangs; it can stalk people; it's a giant creature. It's like a ninja. It hunts the whole crew and eats them all. "Alien" became "Aliens," which was the sequel directed by James Cameron. This is in 1986.

In 1987, there's "Predator." "Predator" involves aliens from another world who come to the Earth to hunt humans as a sport. The alien is very ugly. It's got fangs. He's got a very big mouth and it has weapons. "Predator" has weapons. Then you have "War of the Worlds," which is an invasion from another planet, from Mars, they came here to wipe out the entire human race. All space monsters, right?

"Independence Day" (1996), massive motherships come to the Earth. The creatures wear biomechanical suits with one intention: to blow up, to destroy the Earth and all life on it. No explanation was ever given for the invasion. No explanation was ever given for a massive invasion. Same with the 2011 "Battle: LA."

Now all these movies have sequels. "Alien" has had four sequels plus crossovers with "Predator" and "Alien vs. Predator." "Alien 5" is in the works. You have "Predator 2" in development. You have "Prometheus," which came out in 2012, which is a prequel to these creatures from the other planet. We meet other aliens called the "Engineers" who also want to remove the human race. They're also monstrous.

"Prometheus 2" is being made into a movie. It'll be released in 2017. "Alien 5" is going to come out in 2018 or 2019. "Predator 2" is in development.

All of this is this kind of fantasy with the space monster. The space monster, it didn't come from outer space, but it came from Hollywood because there's no evidence to prove that there's such thing as a "space monster."

The question is: Did the space monster make us afraid of traveling to outer space? One of my theories is that we have stopped looking offplanet, basically, because we are afraid of what's out there. There's the "bogeyman."

The interstellar bogeyman is out there and every incarnation of this bogeyman is terrible. It's a monster. It's a virus. The "Andromeda Strain," right. It's a deadly interstellar virus. It's bacteria. It's a monster. It's an entire race. It's an armada of motherships.

NASA stopped their manned missions to the moon in 1972. We stopped sending people, if they ever went to the moon, we stopped going to the moon in 1972. So are we afraid of space? Is all of this coming from this space monster mythology, this space monster paranoia/ propaganda.

So a few years back I decided to research the space monster and I relooked into all the alien movies because I wanted to find out myself if there was any evidence or was it just my own misperception.

What I did was I decided to take all of the alien movies from the 1950s, which is a good starting point, and I looked until about 2012. The time of the first "The Avengers" movie was released. It was about 2012. In the first "Avengers" movie, the

Third Act included a full-scale alien invasion. Again, we have that alien invasion.

So I looked at 250 alien movies—I watched 95 or 96 percent of them—some of them I couldn't get full access to; some of the movies were older or were harder to get access to. I went through libraries. I got online. I rented movies. I had my own movies. Some movies I watched more than four or five times, even 10 times. I read the reviews. If I didn't get the whole movie, I watched the clips, I read the reviews, I read the production notes (in some cases I had seen the movie as a child). I looked at the cast. I looked at the director. I looked at the director's interviews, you know, I looked at as much information as I could before I formed an opinion and then I gathered my evidence.

What I found was very interesting—we're talking about alien movies, alien-themed movies and these were movies with major distribution, not small budget movies that never made it to the theatres. Movies with an alien theme.

I found that 91-percent of all of these movies, the aliens were evil. They were monstrous. They were evil. They wanted to hurt mankind. Ninety-one percent. That's a strange number, right? What that says is 91-percent of all alien cultures have a bad intention, are evil, are monsters. Ninety-one percent of all alien cultures.

Alien cultures, in my view, as I've discussed many times is that alien cultures are advanced and when you become more advanced, what the movies are saying is you become more evil; and you become more tyrannical; and you become more determined to wipe out societies. That's what the movies are saying.

What I'm saying is when you become advanced, you don't necessarily do that, and you look at any demographic, any culture, you're going to find a variance. You're going to find spiritual groups, you're going to find ascended groups, you're going to find people who are against war. You're going to find a whole spectrum of ideologies and not just one ideology.

Again, this is from Hollywood. This is the movies; 91-percent all the aliens are evil. The other interesting thing I found was that 75-percent of all the movies of the 250 movies I watched, the central theme was an alien invasion. Which supported, actually, my own hypothesis, my own suspicion, that something was amiss, but the evidence proved it. Seventy-five percent of all alien movies involve an alien invasion. An alien invasion involves a full-scale invasion. Whether it involves replicating, duplicating bodies or whether it involves a virus for reprogramming people; it's varied, right.

It's whatever the imagination can concoct. That leaves about nine percent of all alien movies had a mixed intention; some good, some evil intention and when I looked at it closely only a handful of movies presented the advanced interstellar culture with any objectivity. A few movies over the last 65 years.

We're talking about 65 years where the alien has been presented as evil and with the bad intention of destroying the Earth and killing every human being; whether they're into space traveling, which means get out of space or whether they're here, which means we're going to end your life here.

If you go to France, can you say that 91-percent of French people are evil? If you go to Vietnam, can you say that 91-percent of Vietnamese are evil? If you go to Japan, are 91-percent of the Japanese culture evil? If you go to America, are 91-percent of Americans evil? And the answer is, "No." There's no culture where you can say 91-percent of those people are evil, but when it comes alien culture the movies are saying that, whatever alien it is, there's a 91-percent chance that it hates us, it wants to kill us and we shouldn't trust it.

All of this is contrary to what's really going on to the children here, to the benevolent aliens, to the altruistic groups, to the diversity; and cultures that have been here; have been ongoing; have been visiting and haven't destroyed the Earth.

If you look at the history of the Earth, the Earth has never been destroyed. You look at the biblical documents; you look at historical documents; you look at the Earth— look at the Earth, it has never been destroyed. There's never been a documented full-scale alien invasion.

Some people might argue that millions of years ago there likely may have been cataclysmic events, even interstellar events, but is what happened five million years ago relevant to our 21st century society? I don't think so. I don't think people care what happened 50 years ago because it isn't relevant. We have leapt technologically and culturally. I am certain some tragic events happened on the Earth over 4.5 billion years. I just don't lose any sleep over it. Plus, the planet is still here.

So the space monster, the alien invasion, these are concoctions or as I say "propaganda" because it doesn't exist except in Hollywood.

Paris Tosen

STELAN NATIONS

Stelan Peoples are not entirely human. They may look human. They may eat human food. They may wear human clothes, but they're not entirely human. And some Stelans, they obviously don't look human. They have blue skin. They have green skin.

They have tentacles...they don't have tentacles. *Kidding*.

I have seen all kinds of Stelans. I have seen insects. I'm not talking about little insects, I'm talking about humanoid, even higher than humanoid insects. I've seen insects that are intelligent. I've seen Bird People. I've seen people with a beak and feathers. I have seen Stelans that are big. I have seen Stelans that are small and they're kind of gray colored.

Now, a lot of times you think that those are monsters, Paris, those are evil monsters; those are creatures. Well, has anybody ever seen a dolphin? You have seen a dolphin. How many people think dolphins are cute? (raise hand) How many people think dolphins are intelligent? (raise hand) If I told you that a dolphin is an alien what would you say? If I told you a Stelan is a dolphin would you be afraid of dolphins? You wouldn't be afraid of dolphins because you think of it as a dolphin, you don't know it's a Stelan.

I have seen Stelans that are robots, that are not androids but are machines. These are a more advanced kind of Stelan, a cosmic being. I have seen races that are holographic. They are digital, a digital race of people.   Those are also a kind of Stelan. You have the whole spectrum, from the human to the mammal to the interstellar, and you also have under the Earth. You have the Elves in the other dimension. You have a dimensional race, what I call Elves, the interdimensional race.

You say, "Paris, what are the Elves from another dimension?" The Elves used to be called the Pharaohs and all associated High Class of Egyptians, the Pharaohs. I would call them the Elves; the Elves is a new term. The Pharaohs were a race of Elves so let's say the Elves as a species has many races. The Pharaohs were one race.

Okay, what other race of Elves were there? There were the Atlanteans. My research says that the Atlantean's were also a race of Elves. They come from the Inner Earth.   They come from the other dimensions. They're interdimensional. They're advanced. Some people think they had a past life as an Atlantean, or a Pharaoh, or Cleopatra; Nefertiti. These are Elves.

There other kinds of Elves. There are many races of Elves There's a more sprite-like Elf and there's the interdimensional Elf; and there are the Wood Elves, the Elves that live in the trees and the forest.

Those are Stelans.

You see there's a wide variance of Stelans and they're integrated with our culture, with our history, because the Pharaohs were here thousands of years ago. The details of Atlantis are still reminiscent of today. Sometimes the Atlanteans are connected to water or that there's fish people, but then you look at that the mythology, and you understand interdimensional travel, you realize that sometimes "fish" is another way of saying that this guy comes from another dimension. The fish person, the fish people, emerged from the energy of another ocean. They have different colored skin, right?

Sometimes that's also in the mythos, but it's not explained that they come from another dimension because the early cultures maybe didn't understand that. You have the Stelan Nations on the Earth and they have been around for a long time and they have interbred with the local population, the local culture.

In other words, the DNA of the human has a mixture of all these races and the DNA has also been modified. We share 95 percent of our DNA with the chimpanzee. Some people say 98 percent. But if you look at it more closely, it's about 95 percent we share with the chimpanzee. That means five percent came from somewhere else. Five percent made us look the way we look. And five percent could be Stelan DNA or interstellar DNA or the DNA of other beings.

We also share DNA with bananas. You know we share half our DNA with the banana. Whatever is in the banana, half of it we have ourselves. We don't look like a banana. We don't look like a monkey and that's the thing about DNA, you can differentiate between all of these different cultures through small genetic modifications. In other words, the distance between humans and the Stelans can be only us few sequences of genes.

Not only that, it could be a few sequences of genes which we have, which are not activated. Just like the distance between the human and the monkey, the chimpanzee, is five percent of the DNA. If we change that five percent of the DNA we would be the monkey.

If we changed a small percentage of our DNA, we would be an alien.

We would have different colored skin groups. We might look like an insect. We might look like a bird. We might look like anything, so genetically speaking, we are very close to the Stelans (the real Stelans) and we are also very close to our other Primates and the chimpanzee; and we are a little further away from the banana. The banana and the corn.

It wouldn't take much for say an advanced Atlantean scientist to take some DNA from the corn, to take some DNA from a banana, to take some DNA from the monkey and to splice in some synthetic genes and to splice in some Atlantean genes and to create a human. That is *well within* scientific possibility. In fact, our scientists are very close to it right now.

An advanced scientist would be able to do that routinely if you understand DNA. If you are a master of DNA, you've created synthetic DNA, you can synthetically produce the DNA you want to create a designer race.

In other words, to create a human, a human with specific lungs for the atmosphere; with nostrils; with a particularly shaped cranial capacity; with a particular speech complex; and with a particular mix of the hemoglobin in the blood; the particular eyesight/optical capability—you can design all that if you have a good understanding of DNA.

So we have the spectrum of these races that we are all very close to at the genetic level—you know, we look completely different from a banana, right, without showing you the picture, there's a banana and there's a human and we share 50 percent or more of our DNA with a banana.

We share 95 percent with the Primates or the chimpanzees, and what I want to say is we share a lot of the DNA with the Stelans cultures or the interstellar cultures; the Stelan Nations. These Stelan Nations have their own races. They come in different shapes and sizes and they've been an integral part of the human evolution.   The problem is that all of this information is vehemently covered up. When I talk about this stuff they say, "Well, you're not a geneticist, you're not a scientist, you're not an anthropologist, A and B, C is aliens don't exist. You are a nut."

I'm only a nut because this is covered up. Once this information becomes more public, I will not be seen as a nut. We are at a point in history where Stelans are interacting with human beings closer and closer. We have more scientific discoveries; we have more imaginative stories in the movies; we have medical discoveries; we have new ideas, we have the new levels of human rights; we have a renewed interest in space travel; we have some more pioneers; we have a massive development in technology, in computing, in 3-D computing, in holograms and holography—all of this is a result of our race becoming closer to our ancestors who are advanced and who may or may not look human. But just because they don't look human doesn't mean we don't share most of the DNA.

Paris Tosen

CONTACT STARTED 2,500 YEARS AGO

A lot of the reasons why very few people, the general society, mainstream society, why they don't know about interstellar cooperation or interdimensional cooperation is because most of the things that have been happening have been happening behind-the-scenes. There are a number of reasons for that. There are some good reasons and there are some bad reasons. The good reasons are that human readiness has not reached that level where a Stelan culture, a genuine culture can properly interact with mainstream society or the public.

Imagine if an 8-foot-tall insectoid being, an insect being were to walk into a mainstream mall, a large, famous shopping mall, how would society react? And the answer is very obvious: a) Society would not react in a positive way. b) The media, which is easily controlled and manipulated by these intelligence groups and the master controllers, they could spin this kind of intense scenario, as an example, into the most incredible threat in the history of the human race.

Any genuine interaction, without human readiness, would impact the public at large and could be spun and twisted and used as another fear campaign, as another threat, which would be evolved into some kind of intergalactic threat and the whole human race is all of a sudden in trouble.

That brings us to the second reason. The second reason is there's a lot of this negative anti-alien propaganda which has been ongoing for 65 years. Why doesn't the public know about interstellar cultures, Stelan cultures (Stelan Nations), because the public isn't ready and because there is a lot of negative propaganda.

Within that propaganda there are other things that are contending for the human acceptance; things such as religious beliefs or beliefs about spirituality; the beliefs in a divine being; cultural beliefs, practices and traditions, expectations.

You're also competing with what's important to society things like having a job, paying the mortgage, bearing children, becoming successful in life; for some people becoming famous for the sake of being famous, to be recognized, to be appreciated, to discover something no one is discovered.

Most of society, their focus is on these things. The last thing they're thinking about is if there's some alien mothership hovering over the Earth, so there's no interest.

Also, you add to that the propaganda that says that if there are aliens 91-percent of them want to kill us and most of those will want to do some full-scale invasion at some point. You don't want to know, so people don't want to know. The Stelan societies said, listen, we need to contact human culture at some point. We need a reconciliation.

It's just a natural process of human progress. It's a natural process of a civilization to meet their ancestors just like any family. When you grow up, at a certain point you want to meet your long-lost grandparents. You want to research your ancestry—who was my grandfather, who was my grandmother, who were their parents. What is my bloodline? What kind of family tree?

It's a natural human characteristic and more and more people are looking into their ancestry. "Oh, I was related to this person and this person." On a larger scale, human beings, they have ancestors who come from other worlds and are offplanet.

Again, it's important now because the Stelan demographic, according to my research, is that anyone under 25 years of age is 100-percent Stelan; therefore, their ancestry, their DNA, although has human characteristics and their parents also have their characteristics within that DNA; there is additional DNA that comes from offplanet and is significant enough that they should be aware that they have a different cultural background. That goes back to the chimpanzee being 95-percent human and we are 95-percent chimpanzee. But if you look at the human and chimp, they are completely different, except five percent.

Human and a banana are 50 percent same. The human has 50-percent banana DNA and the banana has 50-percent human DNA. The look is different. The Stelan generation—what I call Generation Stelan, 25 and under—twenty-five and over, people do have Stelan characteristics and offplanet DNA and there are mixtures of other genetic influences, but not 100-percent and in varying degrees across the world, so it's a larger discussion.

What I've been focusing on is that I can say that the under 25's are clearly Stelan. That means their ancestry is also offplanet. How do the aliens, the interstellar cultures, how do they communicate with their offspring, their children? Or the children that they have helped to evolve to some degree through the human parents, how do they communicate, given the situation of propaganda and cover-ups? There is no government support. There is military interference. There's intelligence disinformation How do you communicate?

Human beings are afraid of aliens, but the children are not afraid. Most children understand what I'm talking about. A younger child will understand what I'm talking about. They will have seen different kinds of people. They will have different kinds of experiences. They will have different kinds of intuitive responses and I've seen this up close myself.

I have been in a coffee shop where a 10-year-old girl looked at me and she knew that I wasn't of this Earth, and her mother was there frantic. You could see she hadn't slept for weeks. She doesn't know how to deal with this child who sees Star People. I decided not too the ruin that woman's life (that time), but the child understood.

I've been in coffee shops full of adults who don't know the difference between right and wrong, I mean they have no idea what's going on. The young generation, although not all of them are talking about it, they understand what I'm talking about. They understand that there are people off planet. There are people that come through the walls. There are multidimensional people. There are people with green skin and blue skin and orange skin. They understand it, so it's funny for me because when I talk to younger people they understand what I'm talking about. When I talk to adults, they just make up stuff, they start talking about disinformation. They start talking about UFOs. They start calling me names. There is quite a discrepancy.

My focus is on the young people. I want to talk to the people under-25 because they understand what I'm talking about. They're willing to understand what I'm talking about. The Stelan cultures decided, listen, we have these issues, but we need to communicate to the next generation. They have some information going through, people like me talking, for example, but they've also done other things.

What they've done is they're raising the level of science. They're raising the level of medicine. They're raising the level of food quality. More people eating organic, natural foods. They're increasing the level of knowledge and education. They're increasing things like human rights so that we don't discriminate. If you can't accept somebody for their gender, you're not going to accept somebody from another planet. If you can accept someone's gender and racial tendencies and skin color, then you're more likely to accept interplanetary beings.

It's part of that process. It's part of the progress of the civilization. Discrimination, racism, well, if you're against the certain color of people then you're against blue-colored people, for example.

All of these changes are happening. The technology which we have, these smart phones and this software, is changing and we're having more and more holograms; and were having more and more robots. Now there are some negatives. I don't focus on the negatives as much as other people. There are some issues with the negatives, but we have artificial intelligence and robotics and holograms and they have benefits. Genetic engineering has a benefit.

Again, all these things can be used for negative purpose and I'm not saying there aren't negative, darker alien groups. This has been an ongoing issue for a very long time and most of those are in high positions of power. Most of those are very powerful and rich people. They look human. That's an ongoing issue.

My issue is the young generation, now, born in the 80s, their genetic disposition, their genus is Stelan. Their appearance is human.

The genuine Stelan cultures want to communicate with them on an increasing basis and within my lifetime we are going to meet Stelan cultures. Within my lifetime, you're going to meet a variety of interstellar cultures, people from offplanet, so this is going to happen. The younger generation is going to have an easier time with it because they probably know about it. It's in their genes. "Oh, that's weird." The "Star Wars" generation. That's cool. That's weird.

The older generation, you're going to see different reactions especially people who are not educated, especially people who have serious beliefs that challenge new ideas, so contact has been happening for a long time and is leading to a final reconciliation, but it's been ongoing, just behind-the-scenes.

THE STELAN SPECTRUM

The Stelan culture, the young generation today, the new generation is an incredible new addition to the cultural Diaspora on the planet, but it is also a kind of an advanced culture. It can be a perplexing culture and it is worth talking about the basic types of Stelans.

Now in terms of types of humans, I've catalogued a number of types of humans. Today, I'm only going to talk about the three types of Stelans. There are other types of people that I have catalogued that may or may not be in any biology book. I think in the future it will be of importance.

The three kinds of Stelans are: The Activated Stelans, the Hybrids, and the Authentics. Three kinds. Within these three kinds there is a large variance because you can have different levels of activation; you can have different kinds of hybridization; you can have different Authentics with a different cultural heritage or a genetic lineage or bloodline. We do get variances. I just want to make clear that this is not all cut in stone.

Plus, I am not a geneticist.

ACTIVATED

The Activated are children or people with Stelan DNA (interstellar DNA). The interstellar DNA is turned on to a certain extent; is activated.

Activated means the genes are turned on or the gene sequence has been turned on. Now, some gene sequences are tied to the age of a person. As a person becomes older, as they reach puberty, and adolescence, and adulthood, those genes—those natural human genes turn on and also those Stelan genes which are associated with those genes, they get activated. That means that when a Stelan child reaches puberty they may have additional issues, we'll talk about that.

They may have more sensitivities. They have more intuitive responses. They have more levels of intelligence. They have more issues to deal. There's an activation. Although it can be tied to age, activation can also be tied to cosmic energy. Let's say cosmic energy is any energy that comes from the outside of the planet. From the sun or from another star system, even from another galaxy. That energy, this stellar energy, hits different molecules in the atmosphere and activates those molecules and those could activate genes; within a Stelan. An activated Stelan.

A cosmic shift could change a person who has those genes. I think it makes a lot of sense. Who has those genes can be the discussion. Again, anybody under 25 may be more sensitive to these cosmic energies, with the electromagnetic energies of the Earth, as the Earth is shifting.

When Earth is at a low point, you might feel more depressed. When Earth is at a high point, you might feel more energetic. You might feel more courage. You might feel braver. It's not as much of a "I am depressed" as much as the Earth is going through a phase and I am connected to the Earth; and therefore I am feeling it.

The human culture attributes all of their ills and headaches and moods according to they have a problem. It's a personal problem. He has depression. He has a mental illness. He hears voices.

The advanced species, because the genes are connected to reality and to the planet, and to the universe—it's going to become a big discussion because eventually we have to talk about the nature of reality, but I can't get there at this point.

You are connected to the Earth. A Stelan is connected to the Earth. If the Earth changes you're going to feel that. If you become older, if you go through puberty, you're going to have different kind of feeling. When you go through menopause you are going to have a different kind of feeling. When you get older you have a different kind of feeling. I've tried to simplify it. Because these are lengthy discussions that I've written and discussed in other videos—I've written about this extensively.

The Activated Stelan has additional interstellar DNA, however you want to classify it. We have to find some common "terms" so we don't start making up stuff about Martian DNA. Stelan DNA.

HYBRID

The second type is this Hybrid. The Hybrid is a created person, usually created in a lab. Created means they take some human DNA and then they take some interstellar DNA, they may even take some synthetic DNA, and they create a new kind of person.

A new kind of person means: through normal breeding, with two people breeding, you cannot create this kind of person. So this person is kind of like a Hybrid. I think more and more people are familiar with the term "hybrid." And I have personally met Hybrids and they are different. They're very different and I think we have to learn to be sensitive to the fact that there are different kinds of humans living together. Some of them are more sensitive. Some of them more shy. Some of them can even be more outgoing or outspoken. They have all these characteristics.

The Hybrids, I have met Hybrids, they are very different and they are here. Some people are Hybrids. Again, you could, you could have a Hybrid with more synthetic DNA. You can have a Hybrid with less synthetic DNA, with certain levels of activation.

The base quality of a Hybrid is a distinctly different kind of race whereas this Activated Stelan is mostly human with significant Stelan DNA.

AUTHENTIC

The third basic type is the Authentic Stelan. The Authentic Stelan is a human that is from offplanet such that the significant portion of their human DNA is from offplanet. They are basically alien.

Again, I'm not talking about one or two people who have this. We're talking about thousands, or millions. In the movies there's one alien guy, or alien girl, and everybody's chasing that person, but that's not the case anymore.

There's millions of all these people. There's millions of Activated Stelans. There's millions of Hybrids. There's millions, even tens of millions of Authentics, to identify one or two is kind of pointless because they are all over the place.

An Authentic Stelan, which means that their DNA comes from offplanet, which means that they could've been born on a mothership; they could've been born on other planets; they could've been brought to the Earth; they could've migrated here; they could've migrated here as a young child. Any kind of these scenarios where the child with a genome that is from offplanet, they're very different. Again, DNA in human beings tend to assimilate pretty quick.

Human beings are an adaptive species. We have survival skills. We have instincts. All of these things come into play. The human being itself, again, migrated here at some distant point.

My understanding and my belief is that a long time ago all these things were ongoing. Some human beings migrated here from other worlds. Some human beings were genetically engineered with the local primate culture and other animals. Some human beings were engineered in a lab.

Because scientifically we can do that now and scientifically the Stelan cultures could've done that 5,000, 10,000 years ago. The fact that I'm discussing this now, I'm just covering what we forgot because this stuff happening now is not a new thing. It's a protocol that happens across the universe.

You go to a planet. Some people migrate to the planet. When you migrate you need more people, so you start to genetically engineer some of the inhabitants and use the local DNA of the primates, of the animals, and you decide, well, we need some other people so we'll create some other people in the lab.

For these reasons, for survival reasons, for the reasons to protect them against bacteria, viruses, whatever the reason, it's just—it's a scientific protocol. So these three kinds of Stelans, and there are other types of people which I'm not going to discuss here, but I've discussed elsewhere.

There's three kinds of Stelans and within these three kinds the types of hybrids can be very different, and there are differences between the genders, and when you get these different kinds of people, you get these different characteristics of a human being. People more sensitive to energy; people more connected to the Earth; people who are less violent; people who don't identify with their gender. We think it's a human belief that it's connected to your genetic disposition that you, you may have a different heritage.

Your gender association, whether or not you want to have children, your contribution to society, your activism, your willingness to speak out on certain issues, to represent certain underclass citizens, you're interested in writing extensively, making certain kind of films, becoming an artist. Your health challenges, you might be more allergic to certain foods. You might be allergic to nuts. You might hear voices. You might see things. You might talk to ghosts. You might have an interest in the cosmos, cosmic thinking. You might have some gift; you might be a prodigy.

All of these characteristics, I think, are the characteristics of these modifications and these changes in the Diaspora of the human culture, which has been happening for a long time. It's just in the recent 25 years or 30 years, it has accelerated to such a point that now we're seeing the results of those shifts. My interest is that these people need to know that there are different types of people, genetically speaking, even though science hasn't proved it yet, even though it hasn't been officially sanctioned, even though some people say, "Well, you're not a geneticist, what do you know?"

I know this because I am in contact with these Stelan People. I have a deep relationship with these people and I have been watching and studying, for the last 10 years, society, and the shifts. And I have met Stelans, all kinds.

I have met Hybrids and I've met people who have had offplanet DNA. And I've met other kinds of people. I'm speaking from experience and my own research; and all of this information is not always getting to society and if it does get to society it's always fearful propaganda, disinformation.

Paris Tosen

CONCLUSION
THE ARRIVAL OF STELANS

The relentless negative characterizations of "aliens" and "extraterrestrials" in mass-market novels, big budget horror movies set in space, and serial television shows has woefully implanted a barrier to genuine interstellar contact. This dissemination of false truths and evil caricatures has far worse weakened the true history of humanity. The result of all of these psychological machinations has produced a 21st century people who still do not know their true origins. Worse, they still have not had that "UFO Disclosure" they were promised.

While the actions of the past are hard to change, even harder to find those responsible, this hypnotic process and censorship need not continue. Today's generation, and all future generations, have every right to have their secret histories revealed. If not, we will not evolve as a civilization and will remain mired in stagnant ideas, ridiculous knowledge, and falsified facts.

The necessities of the past belong in the past. The truths, I argue, need to be released from their unlawful and un-rightful sequestration. Some of these truths I have shared from my point of view, as a summary of what truly happened because the true history of our planet is bound up in the suppressed information on extraterrestrials. I've offered a start, a quick look at the way things really work.

The real process will be more involved and will coincide with the appearance and arrival of Stelans. That will launch a reconfiguration of the world. But that remains in the nearby future. For now, I have offered a summary of things to come. Dismiss them, debate them, or discuss them—my experiences with genuine Stelan cultures have taught me these things and these things are important because these are things every human has the right to know.

INDEX